Ham
the Astrochimp

Ham the Astrochimp

Written and illustrated by Richard Hilliard

BOYDS MILLS PRESS

HONESDALE, PENNSYLVANIA

ALONG TIME AGO, a baby chimpanzee was born in Africa. His name was Chang. Later he would have a new name, one the whole world would know. As he slept, cradled in his mother's arms, he never could have dreamed of the adventure that lay ahead of him.

When he was old enough to leave his mother, Chang and other chimps were brought to New Mexico. There they would be trained to do something no other chimp had done before—travel into space as part of America's Project Mercury.

Chimpanzees, like gorillas, orangutans, and gibbons, are not monkeys, but apes. Apes are more like human beings than any other animal, and chimps are more similar to us than any other ape. Their skeletons and internal organs, as well as the way they respond to commands, made them ideal test subjects for the final set of Mercury space capsules that flew before the astronauts took over. There were too many unknown factors to place a human in the capsules at first, so NASA scientists decided to send chimpanzees instead. Today, many people think it was cruel to send animals into space, but the chimps were able to obey commands and perform simple tasks, providing an important step in humanity's first voyages into space.

Chang was renamed Ham, in honor of
Holloman Air Medical Center, where he was
trained. Of all the chimpanzees at Holloman,
Ham was one of the brightest and had a great
personality. This was important, because if he was
chosen to go into space, he would do so without his
trainer at his side. No one knew if living creatures could
function in the vacuum of space, so scientists at NASA decided
to test a chimp before they sent a human being into the unknown.

Edward C. Dittmer Jr. was Ham's trainer, as well as that of the other chimps at Holloman Air Medical Center. Ed was born in Laverne, Minnesota, in 1918 and was an army air force aeromedical technician when he came to Holloman in 1957. He worked on many aerospace projects, studying the effects of acceleration and low-gravity conditions on living creatures, and was chosen to train the chimpanzees selected for the early Mercury test flights. Ed was responsible for evaluating the performance and personality of the chimps. He found Ham to be at the top of the class. Ed Dittmer retired from service in 1973, after seeing the success of America's space program firsthand.

America was not the only country striving to put humans in space. Russia, then known as the Soviet Union, was working night and day to become the leader in human space exploration, with the ultimate goal of dominating the United States. The sometimes bitter competition between the two countries became known as the Space Race, which started in the 1950s with the first successful orbits of satellites from both countries. Who would be first at each new achievement became a matter of national pride and national security. However, putting a human in space was no simple matter. Many scientists feared it might be impossible because of the lack of gravity and changes in pressure during launch and orbit. Some even feared that eyes and other organs would stop working in space, so mission officials decided to send animals into orbit before taking the risk of launching human beings. In this fearful climate, people accepted the idea of testing chimpanzees to achieve these goals. With each passing test undertaken by the two countries, it became clearer and clearer that humans could explore "the final frontier."

Moving from New Mexico to Florida, Ham was chosen to be the first truly intelligent being to ride an American rocket into space. On January 31, 1961, the three-year-old chimp was fitted into a little pod, called a biopack, that would sit in the human-sized seat of the Mercury capsule. After engineers made sure that the capsule and rocket booster were ready, Ham blasted off into the sky!

Ham was the first chimpanzee to travel into space, but he was not the first animal to ride a rocket. Fruit flies, mice, and many different kinds of monkeys took the earliest test-rocket flights. However, their aptitude could not help answer the question of whether an intelligent creature could make decisions and perform tasks in space quickly and without difficulty. The Russians found some answers with Laika, a dog that was the first animal in orbit. However, she was not trained to follow commands like a chimp. Ham showed that space travel did not limit brain function. A second chimp, Enos, orbited the earth in November 1961, further proving that human beings could survive the rigors of space. Since then, animals have continued to journey into space, with frogs, cats, fish, turtles, rats, and many other species joining Ham, Laika, and Enos as space pioneers.

Unlike the future astronauts, Ham did not really fly the capsule. Instead his hands worked little levers that scientists could monitor back on Earth. They made certain he could follow directions, see clearly, and make decisions quickly in the weightless environment. As the capsule radioed signals back to their command center in Florida, the NASA team looked carefully at the control panels. It was clear Ham was doing everything he was trained to do as he flew faster and higher with each passing second.

The Redstone booster was not powerful enough to push the capsule into a full Earth orbit. But as the booster separated from the capsule, Ham reached the edge of outer space. Blinking lights told Ham which levers to pull, and he completed the tasks just as he had during training. Every time he was successful, a little treat would pop out of the front of the biopack for him to eat. With no window to look through, Ham had no reason to be frightened by his flight, even though he was miles above Earth. Just like Ham, the capsule was working perfectly, proving to the scientists that it was safe for future human flights.

The first American space flights rode Redstone booster rockets into suborbital space. The Redstone was originally designed as a surface-to-surface missile and was not powerful enough to carry someone into orbit. Atop the Redstone booster sat the Mercury space capsule. The capsule was designed to carry a single astronaut into suborbital or orbital space, supplying the occupant with adequate life support to sustain launch, orbit, and reentry. Reentry could be dangerous because of the friction that built up on the spacecraft as it fell back to Earth. A heat shield on the bottom of the craft protected it from burning up. Enclosed on top of the capsule were radio equipment and the giant parachute that would gently lower the capsule after reentry.

Ham's Biopack

Meanwhile, Ham's capsule was going faster than the engineers had calculated. This meant he would be in space longer than planned. Ham would be weightless for 6.6 minutes rather than 4.9 minutes. It posed no danger to the little chimp, but it meant that his capsule would not land anywhere near the target. Planes and ships in the Atlantic Ocean would have to scramble to find him once he returned to Earth.

After the almost twenty-minute flight, the Mercury capsule landed safely in the Atlantic, but no one was there to see it. Ham was more than fifty miles away from the nearest ship, and his capsule began to leak. Every second mattered as gallons of water started to collect inside, threatening to carry Ham to the bottom of the ocean, where rescue would become impossible.

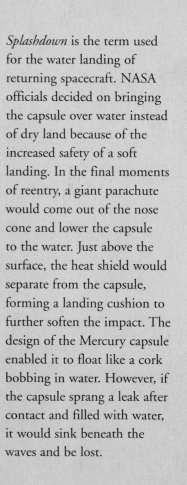

Splashdown is the term used for the water landing of returning spacecraft. NASA officials decided on bringing the capsule over water instead of dry land because of the increased safety of a soft landing. In the final moments of reentry, a giant parachute would come out of the nose cone and lower the capsule to the water. Just above the surface, the heat shield would separate from the capsule, forming a landing cushion to further soften the impact. The design of the Mercury capsule enabled it to float like a cork bobbing in water. However, if the capsule sprang a leak after contact and filled with water, it would sink beneath the waves and be lost.

Although not as fast on the scene as an airplane would have been, the U.S. Marine helicopters used for spacecraft recovery were able to get to the site more quickly than a ship sent to search a wide area. Of greater importance was the ability of the helicopters, also called choppers, to lift the capsule out of the water by attaching a cable to its nose. Once the astronaut exited the spacecraft, the capsule was pulled out and taken to the closest navy recovery ship, where it was lowered to the deck. After the capsule was secured, it was carefully inspected and studied to aid in the success of later flights.

Nearly thirty minutes passed before an airplane spotted Ham's slowly sinking capsule. It took almost three hours for U.S. Marine helicopters to arrive and lift the spacecraft out of the water. Over four hundred gallons of water had leaked in, and the officers had no idea what the chimpanzee's condition was.

Once the capsule landed on the deck of the USS *Donner*, officers rushed to remove the hatch and look inside. Ham, the world's first astrochimp, was safe and glad to see the sunlight. For his reward, the men gave him an apple and half an orange, which he ate happily as news photographers took hundreds of photos.

Waiting for Ham on the deck of the USS *Donner* were many news photographers ready to take his picture. As the flashbulbs popped around him, Ham had no idea that he was to become America's first space celebrity. Featured on magazine covers, in newspaper articles, and on TV, Ham became a household name and a symbol of America's growing confidence in its space program. His good nature and friendly personality made him a media star, up to the point when the astronauts would dominate the world's newspapers.

DAILY

ASTRO
HAM IS

BACK FROM SPACE - Ham, the Astrochimp

NASA Engineers plan for manned laun
thin months, says director

The astrochimp became a worldwide celebrity and was featured on television and many magazine covers. But more importantly, Ham proved that intelligent creatures could go into the great unknown of outer space and return safely. America's manned space program was finally underway.

Moving Ham to the National Zoo not only meant that average people could see the famous space traveler, but it also allowed scientists to monitor his long-term health. Ham proved that intelligent beings could function in space, but scientists did not know if there would be any adverse effects from his journey, after returning to Earth. Researchers were happy to find that Ham remained in excellent health long after his flight, and he showed no unusual signs of aging. Unfortunately, Ham was kept alone during this period of study, and he became lonely after so many years of close contact with people. After it was determined that he would remain healthy for the foreseeable future, the researchers allowed Ham to move in with other chimps.

After the excitement of Ham's journey, he was taken to the National Zoo in Washington, D.C., where he lived for seventeen years. Thousands of adults and children visited him there, but he grew restless. He was kept in a large white cage by himself with only an old tire hanging from the ceiling to play with. People saw how unhappy he was and decided to move him to a new home.

At the North Carolina Zoological Park in Asheboro, Ham found a home where he could play outside in the trees. He spent the rest of his life there as a member of a large colony of chimpanzees. Ham is buried at the International Space Hall of Fame in Alamogordo, New Mexico, near a giant American flag.

The International Space Hall of Fame was established in 1976 and recognizes those who have made an important contribution to humankind's exploration of space. Although only human beings are eligible for induction into the hall of fame, Ham's contributions have not been ignored. He is buried in a place of honor on the grounds of the museum, where visitors can pay their respects as they tour the exhibits of manned space flight. Museums such as this are the keepers of the history of space flight, preserving the artifacts of our exploration of the cosmos for generations to come.

Ham was America's first pioneer in space exploration, and his short flight paved the way for the historic missions that came later—from landing on the Moon to the construction of the International Space Station and beyond. Ham's bravery and good nature were an inspiration for all the space travelers who followed in his footsteps.

For Adrienne, who loves animals above all

Special thanks to
Vincent Di Fate; Ted and Betsy Lewin; Murray Tinkelman; Joyce Burns;
and Roger D. Launius, Ph.D., chair, Division of Space History,
Smithsonian National Air and Space Museum

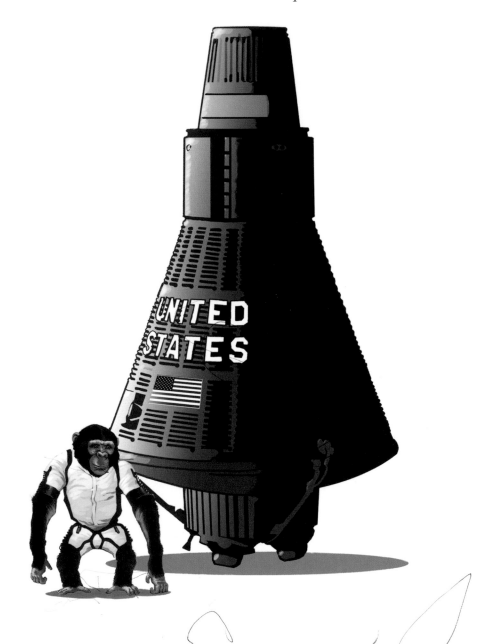

Text and illustrations copyright © 2007 by Richard Hilliard
All rights reserved

Boyds Mills Press, Inc.
815 Church Street
Honesdale, Pennsylvania 18431
Printed in China
www.boydsmillspress.com

First edition, 2007
The text of this book is set in 12-point Garamond.
The illustrations are done in acrylic.

10 9 8 7 6 5 4 3 2 1

Library of Congress Cataloging-in-Publication Data

Hilliard, Richard.
    Ham, the astrochimp / written and illustrated by Rich Hilliard. — 1st ed.
        p. cm.
    ISBN 978-1-59078-459-4 (hardcover : alk. paper)
    1. Ham (Chimpanzee)—Biography—Juvenile literature. 2. Manned
space flight—Research—United States—Juvenile literature.
    3. Chimpanzees—United States—Biography—Juvenile literature.
    4. Chimpanzees as laboratory animals—Juvenile literature. I. Title.

    TL789.85.H36H55 2007
    629.4500929—dc22
            [B]
    2006037940